SHADOW AND BONE

POETRY BY PETER LEVI

Collected Poems 1955–1975
Five Ages
Private Ground
The Echoing Green
Shakespeare's Birthday
Goodbye to the Art of Poetry

PETER LEVI

Shadow and Bone

POEMS 1981–1988

ANVIL PRESS POETRY

Published in 1989
by Anvil Press Poetry Ltd
69 King George Street London SE10 8PX

Set in Bembo by Anvil
Printed and bound in England
by The Camelot Press plc, Southampton

This book is published
with financial assistance from
The Arts Council of Great Britain

British Library Cataloguing in Publication Data

Levi, Peter, 1931 –
　Shadow and bone.
　I. Title
　821'.914

ISBN 0 85646 211 X

FOR DEIRDRE

In younger times I joyed in the sun's ray
and wept at nightfall, now in my sunset
daylight begins in doubtfulness, and yet
holy and tranquil is the end of day.

HÖLDERLIN: 'Ehmals und Jetzt'

Contents

Shadow and Bone

Note on Twelfth Night

(Act One, Scene 5, line 238)

for Shakespeare's birthday, 1981

A willow cabin is a shepherd-house
woven like sheepcotes in the high pasture
where nothing was growing but grass and stone,
ewes sweated in the shadow of a wall,
the light silent, the wind never silent.
It is by love I know any of this,
because the shepherd's music is love-songs.
The thin noise of piping under branches
was love, it was not nature or mankind.
And the pure sheep-spring on the mountain-side
was in his time a holy place of love.
I will call this day holy and this place.

For Martin Robertson

When the fresh leaf is gilt and green
and the lark rises in clear skies
poets and scholars of sixteen
open their eyes.

When thrushes sing in the dull west
and woods are deserts of shadows,
whether pleasure or peace is best
nobody knows:

the good, the true, sound among trees
when singing birds play hide and seek:
scholars like simpler tunes than these
and more antique.

Who wear their soul down to spirit
and drown their science in surprise,
and so with clarified eyesight
open their eyes.

Whatever is, is history,
scholars and sages brood above
ebb-tides of time, might almost be
the holy dove.

When human heat and clarity
meet in the gospel of John
the run of time moves all, and they
like time run on.

They hear and suffer time's footfall,
time is tragic in his motion,
fingers the sand that will end all
and the green ocean.

Who were set free, flew away free
from crowded rooms, imagining
starlight in libraries, simply
a bird might sing.

It is the freshest, obscurest
of voices in the wood of love,
of natures and callings saddest
that I know of.

When clouds of leaf die in the air
and the young swan swims out and dies,
scholar and poet old and bare
open their eyes.

Who only live to die and die,
and the white flower, the green stem,
all beauty, all antiquity
have lived by them.

Seven Old Railway Posters

1

The night mail is this yellow and brown light
where a man not young, solid as brickwork
frozen in the hot act of shovelling
whizzes away, and the blue driver glares,
all quite motionless in furnace beams,
all frozen, all design, all lantern light,
all is Venetian, flying architecture
and decorated gateways of iron.
And yet the stooping man laborious
the furnace of his own feeding defines;
the driver a self-portrait, sea-captain,
man of arts and philosopher and king
his soul eaten away behind his face.
A flask of tea, a sore back at midnight.
Passenger, all this hangs behind your world,
it is peopled by godlike undermen.

2

Far away to the north a yellow dawn
fingers lake-water under the tall hills.
A mist the colour of a blackbird's egg
hangs on the cloudy flanks of the hillside.
Passenger, when you wake there you will see
composed pictures moving behind plate glass,
the tufted trees, islands in the lit lake
and wild geese it may be racing the train
fearful of gunshots, unknowing engines.
And all this shall be yours privately
and with no obligation to record.
Only places are human, having names.
Remember this place in the bad time:
it is implied that you live in bad days.

3

The immense breadth of the white waterfall
like a resounding apron crashing down,
the river underneath boiling like suds,
dark in his tweed the watcher on the rock,
in flat cap and plus-fours, a heavy build.
The silver birch and one mare's tail of spray
gleam with glamorous light: is it the dusk?
There is no railway anywhere in sight,
these places are not for the likes of us.
What is this cliff the river tumbles down?
There are such places in the colonies:
here just the sheep in heather, and the grouse.
Nature is vast. It belongs to a few Dukes.
But the old railways, cobwebbing England,
would take you where you might hear the curlew.
He crossed the Pennines only in the war.
Gaze on this place. You will never get there.

4

Ten of us on a motorboat for six,
the red ensign, nobody much driving,
we pass a windmill and a field of corn,
a distant yacht is tacking far behind,
the Broads are broad and perfectly calm.
This is the elegant, sexy future,
waving joy to the artist I suppose:
Joy! Joy! Name of our motorboat.
The water was uncrowded in those days,
no one showed more than just a pretty leg.
The sky cloudless, the surface reflective.
It cost of course, it was a privilege,
the whites, the long dress, and the bathing dress.
The water was uncrowded in those days.

5

Yellow parasol twelve whole feet across,
the shadow violet and still more vast,
the vaster sand is sun-struck and quite calm,
the sea is froth and the sky infinite:
it is an intense blue too bright to bear.
. Boy and girl muscled like professionals
poise in shadow on an acre of towels
dressed in their bathing dresses and white shoes:
not casual, not happy, pretty though.
Summer's a magazine you read in trains.
It is a paradise of artifice,
her mannish contour, that hot parasol,
the empty sky and sand, the remote sea:
passenger, know yourself in these colours:
summer is just a heavy magazine.

6

Far away, but like somewhere close to home.
The long train runs north as the dawn clears up,
smokes along the white cliffs and the calm bay,
a whole day and night out of London
towards the rocks, the salmon and the stags.
Yet scenery that might be anywhere,
you see no heather rocks or salmon pool,
only the low cliff with the railway line.
As if to say wherever trains run
the same low hills calm seas and yellow dawns
await you fresh forever, passenger.
How easily the long train wanders
among those northern rocks where the deer run.
What promise kindles all night in the train?
The ordinary bay, the yellow dawn?
The lie is in your heart, that steaming train.

7

Two farm horses, a ploughman like a dwarf
under a sky huge as Armageddon,
sun-rinse and rain-sweep and mountains of cloud.
No other cloud is so black or so white,
and the sky where they sail is very tall.
They are sun-smitten, they are wind-worried,
the ploughed land is the edge of this planet.
Come with me stranger, you shall walk this place,
you and the stormy sky, the unbounded earth,
two great horses, a handful of seagulls.
Travel by train to the country of spirit
where souls fume higher than the lark ascends,
and you shall be transmuted into earth.

Fall

There is a coldness on the breeze
and the bough yellows in the lime
like leaf by leaf the death of time.
There is a fever in the trees.

Green clouds that fall away and die
generation by generation:
trees like an empty railway station,
a frozen gesture of goodbye.

Now they stand waiting for the frost,
the fall of leaf and the poem
our children will have read to them
because they love what they have lost.

He Considers the Closing Day

All day the bristling carpet of the crop
laps ragged wall beyond ragged wall,
and the woods settle to a trance of heat.

This week I was in London at twilight,
an old Jew in a cold studio
panting like a lizard on a hot rock,
considering warm whisky water-cooled.

They play the flute in graveyards unemployed.
How kind the world is, how tricky it is.

The elderflower's surf throws cream on green,
and pink roses one has wished for the dead
trail out of hedges so aimlessly fresh.
Weeds flower white in darkening streams.
Under the woods among water-meadows
the railway lines bake in a trance of heat.

All architecture and the soul contain
some smells of iron, residues of soot; life reaches one
season and lingers on.
And today's sun is never a fresh one.

Swallows asleep in cold dormitories
skim in their dreams like spiritual things,
dripping pure light like raindrops from their wings.
Year after year swallows nest in my head,
I am pleased to be crumbling and aged,
and stalking among long shadows of trees:
and think when like a swallow I shall sleep
in the rough greenness and the rough darkness.

I will lie with you for a thousand years.

The end of the day has been clear as water,
rustic sunset, perfectly still and cold,
children quarrelling and calling like jackdaws,
it darkens, pleasure sharpens, when one is old.

I recall days that ended like this one
wandering along hedges like a scarecrow,
coming home late shoes soaking feet frozen,
waiting to see the last light really go.

Comme un vieux vin qui rajeunit le sens:
an old friend, an old love in the fire-smoke;
when you are young you think how it ought to end,
how the birds should more musically croak.

How cold the wine is in the grey houses,
the water in field drains, blood in old veins,
what paper thinness of the face in age,
when the eye sparkles like a dying fire
and the blood rages that will die and cool
in villages as empty as a shell.
And all humours, all kindnesses will die,
and the pure faces and the tree-shadows,
the intonation whispers and is gone.
The leaf of life wears like a river-stone
and crumbles to white ammonites of bone.

The sphere of earth wandering through heaven
bathing her rocky crest in air and fire
has crevices of damp and seas of sand,
and mankind lives where mist accumulates
in bottoms and in hollows of the ground,
Rimbaud's wet place of ferns and violets.
The earth alone, naked, washed in pure air
towers like islands in the streaming sea,
and the ground is sea-salted, ocean-washed.
Earth is rampant, rises far out at sea
in islands of pure rock streaming with light.
And all this is the image of mankind:
who swarm in the green places of the earth
and hide their heads from some high brow of rock
coloured far deeper than the rainbow is,
and washed always by rains of moon and sun.

Notes about Pastoral Poetry

I go back to Ovid through Tennyson:
desilientis aquae, words he loved.
The core of Milton and his conscious art
is Latin whispers of the Thames valley,
the roaring and the sighing in the elm.

I have sought dead men in old paperbacks,
Hemingway for foam beard and iceblue eyes,
and Scott Fitzgerald for his slanted hat.
They are not to be found in libraries.

The year had sun. Nobody can complain.
And ten excellent days of turning leaves.
And a few pears ripened, and a few figs.

Abundance is the heart of poetry,
abundance and continual thinness,
the dazzle of the apple and plane tree.

Through a life without extreme
and the soul drowned in a dream
and content with no extreme
we have followed a deep theme
like the swan on the dark stream.

Old love affairs burn on in their ashes,
the sighing bellows bring them into flame,
and then the old fire goes more quickly out.

In hanging woods, so White of Selborne said,
the voice entangled and embarrassed dies,
and weeping in the rebound it replies.

A poem is a ghost, it has no voice,
we walk through it speaking from end to end,
we walk through listening from end to end.

In making chamber music the soul lives
which otherwise would flutter or not live.
I do not know if God understood this.

The wild fruit ripens in the sun and air,
it is the sour sap of the ragged hedge.

Today the sun is silver, it glitters
in mist, the upper sky is hardly blue.

It will not last. It was not built to last.
This poem, this paper, burning to ash.

The year dies weeping, I write by lamplight;
the rain comes drizzling down the windowpane,
between the low sky and the livid green
the air is full of drizzle and loose wind,
old chinking and clinking of winter song
and slight reverberation of yew trees.
I am not free of my old poetry,
and I foresee the seasons it will keep:
the birth of Christ, the orchid opening,
Valentine day, the birthday of Shakespeare
and longest night and dead time of the year
in which all blossom is generated.
All time circles downwards into eros,
the star of twilight in the day's decline.
Poetry has a right to be private.
The soul is truth, it is a word or two
in the long circling and decline of time.
No instrument of music will awake
the joy the soul has or the peace it has:
though it should hang like tatters in lamplight
or brood among starlit unburied bones.

The air was dark and misty before five
when the robin lay dead by the house door,
whose ruffled breast is cold and is quiet
below the wall where I have buried him,
my friend for whom the star of twilight burned.

Soul is the truth as you breathe it away
as the dry tree loses hold of a leaf,
we are immortal nature yet we die,
every stroke of the brush on the paper
says let go to the spirit as rough breath
disperses in the field at midwinter,
and with the spring stirring, the flowering
of the old violet by the shed wall,
winter I love dies as the spring has done,
the long severity has time to die,
and the trees blossoming and the grass long,
primrose in leaf cowslip in the meadow
have influences on the fainting moon.
Immortal by nature, the soul will die,
white meteors are melting in heaven.

Yellowing dark, the melting of the moon.
What is it in the blue air glistening?
It is the morning star of silver light,
it is the star of summer, virgin-born
above our valley and the western hill,
and the sharp-scented leaf in the nutwood.
Sun of reason that rises in the mind,
and then the meadow-lark in heaven sings,
the Muse echoes, light stiffens into stone
and holy mathematics of mankind,
sun of reason arise again in me
and dissipate all shadows in my soul,
clean my tongue with your fire and I will speak,
the star of morning muses in my mind.

I have become melancholy and mild:
our life is early rain and the dusk rain,
like prisoners of the capsizing moon
or winter mist riddled with bird-whistles,
sunset a red scarf or a yellow scarf
while pots of flowers losing their pure tone
in cottages withering and weeping
speak in their language as I do in mine.
It is the preparation of some change,
few and faint gleams are touching the landscape,
sky fallow, sun still gathering to strike.
And the long days of delirious love
cold sediment of August evenings
stretch out and bask behind us and ahead.
Time is an island, round it seasons run:
one sun slowly ascending over it,
slowly descending under the green turf.
Who hope in God shall rejoice in their beds.

Fifty Short Poems

1

Under the rubbish of old lilac leaf
the hedgehog sleeps who will wail at my death.

2

A long day, heavy as a canopy,
and the toad in his crevice in the stone-pile
considers shadows of nettle and mint.

3

What is it in the misty sun-dazzle?
A cliff, pure white with grass cap of pure green,
the Channel bluish grey rumpled with light,
and the buzz of an antique aeroplane.

4

The soul is candle-light guttering down,
like a light-beam enclosed in stony vaults,
and when the stone is broken, it will shine.

5

Mules in a string climbing towards a spring.
The smell of hot herbs on that mountainside.
Clinking of water and chinking of stone.

6

North wind, the end of June, flowers rusted,
rags in the sky, the blackbird has no song.

7

The dawn at midsummer, perfectly still
and the whole sky light blue like a bird's egg,
the one long tongue chiming away time
has the first freshness of a dream of time.

8

When leaf is green and glitters in the light
the soul sighs among roses under trees,
and in sea-pools as dark as snow-water
the soul fumes in the streaming of the blood,
the soul is cold, the body chills with it.

9

His sheep lie about stinking in shadows,
his wailing shepherd's pipe despairs of love,
he recalls songs only the old men sing.

10

Watery architecture, ruined voice,
soul-music in deserts of solitude,
school of light, and of sight, and of delight.

11

In salt quarries and caverns of the blood,
dark grove of bones, the soul is never free,
music pursues it as the waves pursue
the sun that never drowns, and is reborn
and rises as the soul does, dripping fire.

12

The last light has fallen on the old wall,
and for one hour the garden is alight,
one pool of green with flowers of white light
but greener where the rain has sprinkled it.

13

The long continuous roaring and whining
suddenly muted, and the murky light
clarified into dark and gleams of light,
and somewhere out of sight the sun has set;
the foxes are out now in the graveyards.

14

Passion will melt the edges of the moon,
pleasure at dawn brings up the sun stinging,
to scatter the thin voices of the birds.

15

The fuming of the engine is the soul,
waste heat of energy set free from things,
his engine is his soul and in his hand.

16

Cattle of many colours are grazing
in mountains of a few sober colours,
aprons of meadow, small rivers, dark trees.
The sky is multicoloured at sunset.

17

In cloudy glasses the soul sees herself,
fresh strings of music, grottoes of painting,
cloudily as the body sees and hears.

18

Roses ripen like apples but more brief,
cabbages heave a wrinkled head and sigh,
one quarter of the whole earth has ripened,
the icecap is melting in the cold sea,
only the sea's surface is never ripe.
The world is unripe. The soul is unripe.

19

There is something shortsighted about stars
peering from galaxy to galaxy
across so many millions of miles:
poor crumbs of fire and moon-fragment that must
gleam through their infinities of dullness.

20

Shadow in willows and shade under them
and the dry cowpats in the roughest grass
compose an anthem of the soul at peace
while the body has slid into the stream.

21

In sleep the soul recovers her nature:
fragment of Aristotle, who implies
a low view of the soul and her nature:
the soul is only what is done to her,
or hangs reflected in a river-pool.
Nearby the lover with his reed laments.

22

The universe is leaking away light,
my skull leaks light, my bones leak light,
and light runs in my blood and I leak it.

23

Like moss on timber humid fire will creep
on stony ground and limbs of forest trees,
and the sun's fire is running in the clouds.

24

The cat rolls on her back in the shadow,
shows her pink tongue and capers with one paw:
she narrows eyes as green as gooseberries,
her ears twitch, her whiskers speak pleasure.

25

Wave after wave exploring through heaven.
Darkness. The trumpet sounding their retreat.

26

O unlaborious quiet sun unknown.

27

The barley field due to be harvested
glitters and crumbles in the air and sun,
it shivers in the wind as the sea does.
Harvested year by year a thousand years.

28

Death is the silence after music:
the soul is the first tingling of the string
in the beginning and the first freshness,
then note by note it will begin to die.

29

Maybe the soul is simple breath, a life
as gentle and unconscious as a breath,
individual only like a tree.

30

Memory, the cascades of memory,
the smell of leaf, river-water and stone,
in memory only desire is fresh,
falling through rocks in streams and waterfalls.

31

When souls are twinned like angels in the wind
while bodies kiss and twine cool as roses
souls run together, they run to be one,
that is their rest and breath and end of youth,
and life is nothing, death is nothing.

32

Fear the terrible suddenness of love,
it is like a car door slammed on your hand.

33

Most of your life your soul like an old dog
lies alone in shadows, whimpers and dreams.

34

Shall we be joined together in our death
as we lie now with one soul and one breath?
We shall sleep our last creeping breath away
and we shall be deserted on that day.
The sun will die, as we lie we shall die.

35

Together for ever.
In meadows and shadows for ever.
Infinite spaces of the wind for ever.
The soul is the beginning of wisdom.

36

I think our life is a lake of darkness,
refreshed by springs of perfect purity.
Your springs and mine have run into one stream,
and we are thirsty now to drink from it.

37

Souls in rivers of butterflies that stream
on ghost-looking bushes, grey white and green,
and Buff Beauties, apricot, tangerine,
sturdy but languorous, drowning in cream.

38

The body is more resonant than the soul,
which echoes on the body's chanting walls
like music that is free and is not free:
tones that escape and never quite escape
from conversations of stringed instruments.

39

Is there music in stars or Seraphim?
It is the musing instrument of love
underneath some sweet-smelling balcony.

40

He has three wounds in his body of stone.
O where are they? And what are they? Through one
the moon goes in and out, through one the sun,
and the worm dances in the other one.

41

There is no water colder than death is.
It begins as sweat trickling down your skin.
The soul's eyes are wide open, and she crows.

42

His long-winged soul was flying out of him,
his golden blood lacing his silver skin;
a heap of bones and a few broken stones.

43

Wood of the boat in the skin of the sea,
and the sea-tainted breathing of the boat:
and breathing in the body of a lute
and hollow cello, his wooden body.
The wind in the rigging never silent.

44

I can transform myself into a stone,
a river-pebble, an idle sea-shell,
perfectly silent all eternity.

45

Now I need rain: head like a hot stone,
a sky flushed with the pink rose of the moon,
I dream tomorrow's moon as white as bone.

46

Sunrise is the cold Priestess of the Sun
within the holy cloister of whose eyes
the soul soars up to be with God alone.

47

When we have wandered in Elysium
how will we pass eternity away?
Like lovers, soul on soul and breath on breath.

48

Her rivers shall be inebriated
and in her drops she shall rejoice to spring.

49

Fire, hail, snow, ice, spirit of storms
that do the work of God: praise him.

50

It is so dark now under the trees,
leaf by leaf all heaven is mouldering:
beyond the trees a groaning of the wind,
twilight the scattering of silver crumbs;
eagles of dawn will sweep them with their wings.

The Sun

i

The woods are sombre, soon the leaf will fall,
the clouded sky is livid with stormlight,
the sun is glittering in the dark trees;
in his descent the sun is musical
and sings more to the soul than the eyesight,
he dies sparking with holiness and ease;
his tone is darkening among the trees.

ii

Some extreme purity of this blue light
in time consumes away the dying leaf,
and leaf is cold fire-coloured skeleton,
and sun distils away though it was bright;
I like this wasted immortality
that lingers like a smell when the sun's gone,
these cold honeys on which the sun has shone.

iii

The sun drops like a lover on a bed
empty of love, and yet full of freshness,
ruffling and rumpling rose and yellow sheets
while homely glowing love combs his sleek head,
quenches his light and pulls him down loveless
into a house of silence and heartbeats.
One bird alone repeats, only repeats.

iv

The sun will dive, he has stripped off his fire:
in the moon's weakness his ghost will revive,
while streaming airs make earth an ocean bed
and clouds that kiss the sunset must retire
in confused orders, nothing is alive
but this last glittering which is most dead,
and green silence where the sun hides his head.

The Muse of North Oxford out as far as the Pear Tree
is the ghost of Marianne Moore in a straw hat,
people defer to the black straw hat instinctively,
it speaks to the North Oxford as to the New York heart
    like poetry,
civilized people admire old ladies and that is that.

Matthew Arnold was light-headed for lack of a shiny
    old hat
flowering and withering away on Dover Beach:
the footfall of her verses is as subtle as an intimate cat,
his is like pasture grass, melodious and flat,
she was a mermaid all alone but singing each to each.

Being Irish is part of it, but she was not the Irish muse,
that has pink nose and runny eyes, the Boreal Aurora,
proceeds to Mass at seven in the morning, holds severely
    Irish views,
a simple bitter girl the wide brim would confuse,
to my thinking the true muse was our maid Nora.

God has gone down and heaven is empty,
he has lost his angelic choruses
and they are swarming in a fog of stars:
heaven is dripping a rainfall of fire,
his fire is blazing in the thorny trees
of wilderness and the forest waste:
fire in the thorn and the thorn does not burn,
God has gone down into the fire of God
that flowers in the branches of the thorn,
and the tree burns but will not be consumed.
The Spirit chanting in the water-spring
and at daybreak whose light is virginal
lays down God in the fire in the thorn tree,
and the child Jesus trailing swarms of stars
in the dark branches of his mother's arms
and in the ruined cloister of her mind,
whose silence is broken as heaven is
by muttered conversations of music.
But the fire slept in heaven at that time,
when Christmas light sprang from the ragged star
still burning on the edges of the sky,
down into the moist atmosphere of breath,
and air, and mist, and breathing animals,
draping the cave walls and the cold shadows;
and now the child is warm with their rough breath
and heaven sleeps and Christmas is asleep,
because the drum-beat of the dying blood
and the small music of the childish breath
minute by minute light the road to death,
from which no other traveller returned
except Christ with his sober drunkenness
and antique flower of immortal life,
whom we have known, and whom our eyes shall see,

by whom the light of Christmas is lighted.
Starlight was a cobweb on the mountains,
the mountain sheep were silent at that time:
night stringing thin daylight to thin daylight
ran darkly down the folded mountainside
and the nightwind breathed on the shepherds' eyes
where they were keeping watch over their sheep
by lonely woods and water-springs of ice
and rocky streams that suckled their cold sheep
soon as they woke, and strayed with the dawn star
to graze on the rank grass before daybreak,
and move with shepherds on the mountain tracks
among dark bushes and stone-rooted trees
as day broke and the mist was vanishing.
In what dark field of night, and in what hour
foretold by prophecy and holy fire,
over what hill did heaven open then?
Night knows it, and the midnight of the year
knows the dark season of the birth of Christ,
and resurrection written in darkness:
heaven that turns the stars on their slow wheels
knows him and has cried out over the earth:
the Virgin bears a child, light shall increase.
The hungry shepherds hear heaven's music
and angels chanting to them in Hebrew:
which at that time were heard on the cold hill,
and heaven opened, and the spirits shone,
crying to God with blessing and with praise
in psalms of music and in canticles,
and gave glory to God in the highest
and peace among mankind that love their God;
and on the hill the shepherds sang with them,
whose music is the shrill lamenting flute
and painful fires of love consumed away.

The walls of heaven ring,
they hear the angels sing
and the cock crowing when the earth is still,
it is the God of light
falling from heaven's height
that draws the shepherds from the dying hill.

The sky has withered ripe
where the lamenting pipe
haunted the mountainside in simple grief,
and vanishes away
before the star of day,
and leaves no traces but a dying leaf.

The wandering shepherds cry,
and the sun's ragged eye
lingers in heaven where the angels are,
the spirit army of
the God and Son of love
silently melting to a dying star.

The angel has cried out with tongue of fire:
Almighty child, whose breath is heaven's hymns,
let heaven sleep and earthly music sing,
because on earth a time will come to sleep.
Sky's lucifer and Jesse's root and bud,
heavenqueen, daughter of earth and of God,
suckle the spirit child and he will sleep.
Heaven is sleeping in the hands of earth,
the fire of heaven in moist earthy hands:
the milk is running in the mouth of God
as barren images of virgin milk
trickle and drip down heaven's shining stars
which were dreamed in the Sabbath sleep of God.
So in the rustling branches of her arms
the child slept and the shepherds worshipped him:

whose name in heaven is Emmanuel,
God is with us, who is called Christ on earth,
with blessing and with honour and with psalms.
Stars like fruit shook down from the tree of life,
and from those roots refreshed with water-springs
some inmost sap blasted by Adam's drought
mounted from leaf to leaf in one green blush,
until the thirst of Adam was sated.
Tree of white blossom and midwinter fruit
weaving your house of branches and of thorns,
where heaven's nightingale sings at midnight,
and weeping grotto of the God of light,
where everlasting light reigns in darkness
and heaven's powers in the sleep of light,
lay down that fruit of heaven in my hands
which the prophetic shepherds visited
with blessings and with messages of peace,
familiar messages of blessed peace,
learnt in the mountain shelters of their sheep.
Because the star has set over the cave
and our feet have rejoiced along that road
where angels found him and were comforted,
and sang their psalm at that deserted light,
as blinded stars sing on the shores of light,
which are never silent for his delight
who is the God of intellectual light.
Then three innocent kings came from the east,
three wise creatures came out of the daybreak,
three stars in heaven treading tracks of fire,
and Moses like a shepherd in the stars
brought them to Bethlehem where the child was,
and their eyes saw what no prophet has seen:
the grape slept in the branches of the vine,
fire at rest in the green shoots of the vine,
the God of love at ease on the young leaf,
whose angel cried out with a tongue of fire:
Let heaven sleep and earthly music sing.

The walnut tree is a fountain of leaf,
and the plane tree looks uncultivated;
nourish a small hope that it might not snow
until we get in shelter of the trees.
Life has been a long grove of dying trees
and the young ones are darkening with life.
Life is the musical arrest of time.
Some days I dream I might have money,
but I have not: cultivate small hopes,
the gloss of life dripping down from the leaf,
and the plane still sighing to the walnut.

The Rector wrote his sermon in
the dead part of the afternoon,
forgetful of his steaming greens,
and without honey, without scones,
but like a dog felt in his bones
the fog and darkness of the downs
and sour smells of decaying moons.

When Christmas and the dark days are over
the sun blazes in glittering windows,
we lie in pools of sunlight on the bed,
the village lies sprawling in sun-struck mist
the cocks are crowing miles across the mist.
Air smells of earth and of the frosty sun.
All night I dreamed the branches of a tree
and in my hand the smell of freshest leaf,
the sky was the blue seas as clear as paint
which were intoxicated by the trees.
The light extends a little day by day,
and the small birds are chanting for a friend.
It will be their time as it is our time.

A deep snow-bank, a nine-inch icicle.
The wind is blowing the dry snow about
and it ruffles the pure crust of the snow,
snow glitters as the sun goes out of sight,
still the level sunlight pours over it,
the yellow streams and then the shadow-streams.
And life is not a word, it is silent:
the sparrows and finches picking birdseed
and the last sunlight drapes over the shed,
snow is crisper but stone is hoarier.
Something has woken in the dying light
as deaf as life and as silent as snow.
The scenery of spirit has shifted,
falling away in transformation scenes
of silent snow kissed by the silent sun
and places of the mind, airs of music,
drifting from grottoes of the living woods
and from the god of life who is silent.

Robert Lowell Looks at the Cherwell

The little river swirled a muddy brown,
as if it had Chatterton's bones in it;
the February pools flooded the grass,
mating season had exhausted the swans.
Poets were scanty, poetry was rich,
days of the only man of genius
that either of us knows, the Warden thought.
Out of sex and childhood something survived,
the rotting motorboat, the dead quayside,
and the graveyard infested with vermin.
The soot hung heavy on the towers once
that look so ghostly now they scrub them white,
and they still weigh down the drawing-board
or drown head downwards in the wrinkled flood.

Nadia Boulanger Looks at Monteverdi

Zephyro torna. Torna Zephyro.
Two tenor voices nineteen thirty four
blowing about, musical chimney-smoke,
grey ghost and lush meadows and daffodils:
and for a green renaissance in these days
you have to have forgotten everything.
Lived in a flat beyond the Gare du Nord
I visited with nothing in my head
but black music, white paper, scanty pen:
West wind return to us, West wind return,
Monteverdi, my pleasure-ground, spun round,
she had found him when I was three years old,
took a drink on a terrace in the spring sun:
Valéry's widow older than she was.

The Colonel Looks at the Water

Under the high moors in the lush estates
the river-water deepens and runs on,
it gurgles under fresh branches in May
nourishing islands infested with weeds;
the fish lurk in the cool to propagate.
He is the master of his whizzing fly,
and his life-story is to imitate
the characters of grass and of a stone
like some cold-blooded pleasure-loving thing.
He is a monument of transcendence,
all his proprieties fallen away,
his eyes warm as the quietest morning:
he is the distillation of cock-crow,
crisp in movement, old coat smelling of fish.

Alexander Considers the West

When Alexander the last Persian god
lay dying in his youthful vinous sweat
his fever made mirages in the air,
he would have blasted mountains in their snow
and dipped his hissing sword in western seas
to expire like the last flames of the sun,
consuming the French woods to hide himself
in the ocean's extreme ululations.
What a summer season it would have been,
the Greek horses skirmishing down Snowdon,
the island cliff sighing for its freedom,
the Irish reading Plato before Christ:
and yet without death nothing blossoms,
only snow-water glitters between rock.

Mr Levi Considers Whistler's Mural

The Palace expedition was unsound,
the pink balloon was tethered to the ground;
the woods were dark, Venus's pigeons cooed,
they are not food but a pretence of food:
and these travellers never will arrive,
their one wish is to keep desire alive.
The mountains stand blue-headed far away
and the late season dies in the cool bay,
adventurous aesthetes amble at ease
on gentle tracks among the tufted trees.
Shepherd and shepherdess have music-books,
how sinister the architecture looks,
no rabbit runs among the ripening corn
to feed the leopard or the unicorn,
the music of time fades into a trance,
the sea writhes in an intricate dance.
Pagodas where the tea is over-sweet
and domes of nullness feel the dying heat,
in gardens that the advancing dark will smother
white statues love nothing but one another.
How beautiful it all is, and how cold:
the Thames has flooded it, and they are old.

O most sweet sleep, and then to be wakened
by the geese in the field, one tongue of light
licking the window glass as a cat might;
new suns peer over our roofs in the end.
Was alone in the hayloft with my friend,
the sun struck level in my dream last night,
and if the hay was white she was more white,
and the sun stroked our skins. Shall we pretend
that we can sleep all morning in the sun
and the cat settled and our dog Mozart
are in the old hayloft in the sunshaft?
The dream ended what the dream had begun,
day breaks open the sea and pulls apart
wave after wave, and our bed is our raft.

At early light this country is cobwebbed
with ragged strings of birdsong in hedges.
Half awake and in half-light you hear
a bird beyond the birds extending space;
they will melt at sunset dissolving time,
having guarded both edges of the day,
as if a liquid sun ran streaming down
the river of his long limited life,
and the mind's wandering must be recalled
from barren reaches of eternal pools:
eternity brooding over slowness,
and the earth would be as bare as the moon
freezing water-vapour the end of time,
heaven breathe out the spirit of the just
like voices in fresh waterfalls of stars.

Life is failure. Life is failure to live,
success is mockery you can't forgive.
Failure comes slowly, it is dragged out long
like the slow melted tones of a lute song,
through pools of time for happiness and peace
and then the quiet when music will cease.
Your life fails, then your body fails one day,
your mind goes and the soul will melt away.

Spring is in the senses, not in the mind,
the tang of leafgum in the lush meadow
stirs in the ageing senses as they go
out one by one to deaf, mute, coarse and blind,
and as the oldest tree so long inclined
falls in the end and the house of the crow
is ruins, the stormwind of spring also
tears that soul most which is most unresigned
to invasions and privacies of eros,
but the tree full of leaf falls the soonest,
its leaf plundered, its green places opened,
and the wind loots the wind to its own loss;
in the dark season that tree groaned for rest,
and the grass that it shadowed has ripened.

At this time the moist thrush utters his loud
cry in the wizened sunlight in sweet peas,
and cold air tumbles the laborious bees
from shattered roses sunk in their green cloud:
this poem has gone over, all the same;
the brightest honey has dripped off the trees,
the fresh oak leaf was cropped for Hercules,
gardens and woods are a suburban game.
Yet when you wheel the old scene out of sight
the country is convincing and threadbare,
who ever knew it had so thin a skin?
The garden shuffles and whispers at night,
minute dies by minute in the still air,
as spirit dies, and the straw is ploughed in.

Paper face and hand yellow as a leaf:
this thought is rotted with infinities,
the chanting of the mind is cavernous
and the head-bone sings like a vault of stone,
we are sick people, wisdom is Chinese:
the night is drugged, it is one hospital
where the infected blood pounds in the ear,
sighing with obliterated music:
I crave now for the freshness of the stone
and the incised music of instruments,
all things that are consonant with nature,
and the cold pillow of a child of stars,
the scattered twittering of a few birds
and the crowing of cocks over the wall.

The crude breath of the cattle of daybreak
hangs in the coloured meadow of the sky
and lingers in wet grass and river-mist
and in the juicy whistles of the birds.
Then it is day and there is nothingness,
the sun somewhere wades in a pool of light
and a small river floods and meanders,
the light hangs in silence as the mist hangs,
ice crunches in the marks of the tractors.
Not a god, not a song, not a radio.
The earth has shrugged away its ironies:
how to live better, to breathe easily,
the melted stars of knowledge and virtue,
scriptures of English rotted by the damp,
cow-pastures of the cattle of daybreak.
Before the dusk it will begin to snow.
A distant cry set out, it is set free.
It may be this field is visionary
and angel spirits have wept over it.
I have no tears to shed when visions start
and the field is empty of its old thoughts.
Now the snow falls and hardly cares to rest.

5.20 and 5.21,
the dawn is coming up, and village lights
begin to glimmer back at the sunlight:
the sleepless mind has comfort, the soul sings.

5.20 and 5.21,
the evening curtains hang like sky-pillars,
and the clock is the measure of pleasure,
the wireless and the whisky and the dark.

But the minute that time is understood,
the metal clock is ticking in the blood,
we are losing eternity and God.

The praises of God are abundant and irregular.
The earth is cobwebbed with the trickling of water
and the cold air abandoned among pine trees
neither hums nor whistles, it is a mouthless praise.
Chapels alone in grass revisited by nothing but the
    moon
refreshed with wilderness, rotted to the roots with fog
spell out their alphabets of praises and the heavings in
    the grass
receive instruction from daybreak, the praises of God
    are not lost.
Cold metal clangs in bell-towers in June
multiplying syllables of invisible honey
and the veined rock in the mountain naked in shadows
    utters praise.
The bare long back of the sea wrinkles in the light of
    suns
intoning praises to the everlasting successions of God:
to the God of atheism never to be withered away
though the sea should give up its dead and the praises of
    God should be silent
and languages wrapped in tranquillity as they once
    were.

In nineteen one I might have been
an actor in a country scene
of setting suns,
– walk home through shallow seas of grass,
pass time without hearing time pass,
with dogs and guns.

I could have worked in the bazaar
in the great age of the cigar
and worn an opal,
and slept as quiet as a mouse
under the floor of an old house,
Constantinople.

Or lived in 1929
somewhere beside the Uxbridge line,
just out of sight,
we would have travelled up to town
and bought orchids for half-a-crown
and danced all night.

How many pleasures, and it seems
that we are best defined in dreams
of blood and money,
souls creaking like a tree with age,
and muffled in old foliage
that drips with honey.

This is a country without revelation,
generations of summer have spent themselves.
Bent and bundled together like peasants
we trudge through an east wind with our small dogs,
eaten away at the edges by the snow.
Snow moulders on melancholy hillsides,
it lies inside the woods, waxen and white.
Our poetry's old-fashioned like an old
sunset streaming with wizard influences,
that was bitten to pieces by the dogs.
In the bare grove beside the lake you pass
gleams and reflections on the black water.
Some days the sun pale as a fingernail
brushes the surface of the snowy field.
We die when eros has abandoned us.

In nineteen-thirties gardens children shout,
the fields have wooden carts lying about,
in August the elm leaf is dark and tough,
soon in orchards the apples will drop off,
there are still poets too wet to dry up
who use their fountain pens to stir their cup.

Now at bare tables too severe to rhyme
they peer like winter suns for the first time,
or like the muse of 1910 they hover
in airs of autumn; modern verse is over.
The sky is comfortless and it will freeze,
and the brief sun dies out behind the trees.

In nineteen-eighties gardens you can hear
some kind of mechanical dulcimer,
a girl is picking notes out for her friend,
the old poets have all died in the end.
The sun ruins itself behind the wood,
none of the lot of these were any good.

The world goes on murmuring one low hum.
Will there be poets in the world to come?
At dawn and dusk the birds utter their call,
sad and too moving to be magical.
Time passed by England. Cattle rivers shake
their shaded water, where the birds will wake.

The organ groans and Alleluiah dawns,
the Rector yawns, the congregation fawns.
We are in stalls as meek as any cattle,
his reverence in spiritual battle
defies King James's angels in midair,
and Sunday trading, and the Common Prayer.

Time spent in pleasures will dissolve in air
so slowly it lingers as the light does,
mixing the smell of grass and smell of leaf
in touches of ground-mist as the sun falls
mouthing the last of his clear dialogue,
and suddenly the whole wood smells of mint.
The truth of poetry hangs at tree-height,
consumes a thousand stars in one instant,
gives illusions of dampness and freshness,
tree on tree, leaf on leaf inside the mind
as withering fireworks flower in woods,
conjures the rude lark-twitter through rainfall
as if the soul hung ragged in the breath.
When it is spoken it lingers in us.

The nut shrivels, but the world is alive.
There is no life inward of poetry
no eyes behind the eyes inside the soul,
I rumble down like coal into the shed,
clinkers exhausted by the hand of fire
and long quest for a natural silence.
My mind holds unvisited islands,
stirs with marine hunger for horizons
and ominous processions of seasons.
Now the swallows are beginning to go,
in the morning the flowers are too bright,
the runner-beans are taller than I am.
I have no need for other poetry
but the old age and memories of men,
the coldness, the bright sun, in other men.

For Fram and Candia

How fresh and easy came the equinox,
the autumn wedding day of moon and soul
and the sun wading as the cattle wade
in pools of light between the ragged trees.
The sea's dark glitter carries the mind
as lightly as a saint on a dead leaf
to anchorage under hillsides of trees,
rank hedges where the elm is still alive
and the yacht swings and tinkles in the tide.
Clear sun, the heron and the brown curlew
on wet sand in the shadow of the wood:
the wind has withered, the leaf is alive,
and full moon oils the hinges of the year
for *homo*, *luna*, *sol*, their wedding day.
The labyrinth of hedges smells of herbs
the plum ripening to plum-coloured silk
has stunned the self-intoxicated trees,
the fig darkens slowly on the stone wall.
I never had a friend so much in love:
like actors trailing our sad comedies
at last into the light of heaven's eye
and the long balance of his equinox,
we have consumed the all-consuming fire
and we can never turn away from it.
How still the days are, the air scarcely stirs
the lane-dust in the footprints of horses
or the breath of the dying horse-parsley,
or the late sun melting into the leaf.
Not long now, the moon will be rising
bone-white after a lifetime of winters
over the torn clouds and the sea's distress,
the sun slide from a mist into a mist.

Leaf after leaf will drop away in light:
anima naturae, the soul's course
and seeding-ground of time and of the mind,
to wither only in the hand of God
seeking for resurrection in his hand.

In Memory of Philip Larkin

Gardens remembered grow mildewed and shabby
with unswept leaves and autumn suns that sink,
the ghosts of Muses haunt Westminster Abbey
     weeping in ink.

Only in the waste land beyond the city
the sea dies and revives, never grows old,
consumes dawn, consumes dusk without pity,
     heaving and cold,

and constellations saying now or never
and the moon's pauses in her cloudy chase
set off the future on and on for ever,
     infinite space.

At evening in his sky-blue kitchen chair
some poet in the future I suppose
will write his chronicles of fire and air
while the long light gallops against shadows
over valleys and meadows of pure green;
his country's innocent extreme of love
will be one fugue without any regret,
and the stars in his verse shine clear above
the rose-bedraggled wreckage of sunset.
Meanwhile I must from my plain wooden chair
observe the sweetbriar and the deep rose,
foreseeing time dissolve in dying air,
and the extreme of love is in shadows.

What the Rose Said

for Charles Causley

I am the rose of summer nuzzling spring
half hidden in bright green, smelt before seen,
consumed in one breath, withered opening,
a pod of prickles where a rose has been:
when the storm shatters it the thrush will sing,
then by moonlight the nightingale will lean
a dying breast on the dry thorn singing
music as complicated and as clean
as the bird loving, the rose flourishing,
but not what roses or what poems mean,
because the blood corrupted melts the sting
and words die on the tongue, rose unfolding
melts his whole spice in one refreshing fume
which no songbird or poem can exhume.

Poets have had no influence on life.
It is my just fate to be disbelieved,
love is private, it will not last in words,
it must be nourished with private liquors,
love is a poem continually
crying out not to be believed,
it is the chaff of the impure grain,
my poetry has not intermingled
into the secret crying out of love.

For St Catherine's College, 1987

Fireworks whistling for twenty-five years
and a worn out tune like a fag-end
stuck to the lip for twenty-five years,
courageous in the ballroom of the dead.
Jeremy Bentham is king of the dead:
now there is migraine in the house of God,
in Islington the hollow marble hears
symphonies of a thousand metronomes.
Hardly a hundred years old and disused.
In Oxford in the brambles and marshes,
overgrown islands, divided streams,
they were still building yellow colleges
a quarter of a century ago:
flashing with glass, balances of concrete,
very smooth, very yellow, very exact.
A fountain like Versailles, a mile of lawn,
Barbara Hepworth so dramatic here,
so undramatic in the crowded grove
and dusky flower-garden of statues
and big sea-pebbles where the sisters stand.
Hangars where no warplane has roosted
hear music lured from the dead colonnades.
Scholars sift and resift the coloured sand,
and print like parrots in cigar-ashes
delicate traces of their own footsteps.
Wisdom is secular.
Learning is organized energy.
Air, river and stone interpenetrate.
In this republic nothing is sufficient
and therefore the republic is enough:
bricks bake in their neat yellow designs,

the coupling swans have spurned them and moved on.
The elderly consider
the illusion of happiness in this life
like the dull sun that flares in Armagnac.
The young glide away into the green shadow,
down to the emptiest reaches of the Thames,
the living sun on the vast dancing floor.

I prefer old-fashioned countries
that smell of melons as the sun goes down:
fine autumns, heavy snow in the mountains.
The only history is long ago.
Small, backward provinces
where even the roses are not fresh,
they hang their heavy heads
and the trains are slower than the horses.
Only the light is still alive,
the river and the fish in the river.
The light carries a weak smell of the snow.
The field flowers of the deceiving world
float gently over the long grass.
Rock-doves have colonized the stone ruins,
in the hills they use bullets of gem-stone.
I dream only of what I know.
I am as old and as inefficient
and as snow-matted, as lost from the world,
and fit to lay down my disloyal bones.
I smell deeply of roses and of snow.
There are no heroes, all the young poets
are in the cafés of the villages,
those of them that live will be old poets.

All that country is in the eye of death
as the dead chimneys hear it from hillsides.
At dawn one river hisses like a sword
beaten flat by hammerstrokes of blue light,
a silken waterfall sways in midair
and the hull salt-washed white on the dark bay
is lifted with the breathing of the sea.
The tide runs in, flashing over the sand,
sun flashes in the sand and in the tide.
The irons of the bridge suddenly bent
go stalking step by step across shallows,
crowds of children like flocks of shy seabirds
run through the seaspray, haunt or disappear.
Stray inland and the country becomes green
from the cold breath of mountains and the rain,
and it was Death that contemplated this.

Immortality heaving in the mist,
the white roses, disturbance of spirit,
the hanging wood is one dark silhouette,
quiet of heart, coldness of the rainfall
when wine and gale enliven the thin blood,
then all autumn's one lighted, brief process:
Europe, the diminution of the sun
season by season, never to be young,
hoary antiquity, the mind's refuge:
and when the sun is crisp and underground
dreams of that eastern star that was ashes
before the host of heaven had burned out;
now dawn, stony and speckled as the moon
requires those ashes from the bird of dawn.
That ash has been dispersed, the star is gone:
there is natural immortality
and the nature of God is in nature.
The birds of dawn and the moon's bird cry out
over the clear sea and far overland.

A gale of wind shakes rooks out of the trees,
the rain complains, a wind as raw as life
strips off poems from the darkness of days,
they are too rambling for light's brevity,
that weak blue flaring of the shortest days.
It is winter, flowers have dried and died,
summer's thoughts lie rotting like oranges,
it's goodbye to the themes of poetry.
Camera crews with frozen fingers crouch
under Stonehenge, dawn glows like cinders
summoned up by the cold despair of eyes.
So grain by grain my monument corrodes:
there is no architecture without grief.
The summer daylight lingered eighteen hours
and the priest of lamplight had not been born,
then among trees the common nightingale
sang in his screens of perpetual leaf,
woodsmoke was whiter and the night more black,
earth clod heavy, the stars as sharp as salt,
hedges rough but infinitely scented.
I never was at home in that country:
learn the queer music of the radio
and never trouble heaven if you hear
trees fizzing with the whistle of small birds.
You may stand ankle-deep in the dark lake
to lick reflections, but not undertake
the sobriety of the deserted sea.
We are lost in mid-ocean of our lives,
and the sea-pebbles and the khaki sand
are distant, and the sounding surf distant.

A rook of velvet in a sky of blue
drenching a field of grass when it chooses,
sunlight too innocent to continue:
as if the world were immortal symbols,
unwritten poems the breath of the earth,
and the twang of unlikely instruments,
all the boredom of history, ended where
the silent rowing of a glossy rook
slid to the ruins of a dying tree.

Those that have screwed the most out of their life
enjoyed mouthfuls of sweet milk and dark earth,
they never shivered when death slid his knife
between their ribs and brought coldness to birth.

Their day burnt low and even like a flame,
their memory is clinkers of old coal,
we others shake with envy all the same
taking death's oyster-shell to be the soul.

In the communications of mankind
hand touching hand at the wild end of the dance,
built sturdily, silk-skinned and unrefined,
with the dumb eyes of angels they advance

while we retire, our drooped, innocent eyes
look guilty, yet we linger hand in hand
and in their death, their passion, their surprise,
understand what we sought to understand.

Gin and failure feed the abrasive mood.
Shouting at waiters, roaring in offices,
flashing their damned lights on the dangerous road
they howl hellbent for the last precipice.
People like that will die quicker than us.

I'll never be Darby, you'll never be Joan,
but we shall linger all night, not like those
children of eros, lovers of freedom,
whose soul comes to a slow, musical close.
People like that will die quicker than us.

Suddenly overtaken by the dark
some never notice life or heaven pass.
They can just hear the thin tune of a lark
sprinkle on acres of sun-polished grass.
People like that will die quicker than us.

For Matthew

The woods are stretching, they sway out of bed,
drape shadows and reflections in the stream:
the railway bridge is hanging in the stream,
the long valley slides down into the stream
where willows trundle slower than the train
and the loose echoes flung behind the train
from tree to tree drop silent like the train.
It is the image of advancing time
that stays and never stays and for a time
is noisy and then silent for all time.
The egg of stone is ticking in the clock,
the cuckoo has got free out of his clock,
the railway lines run home into the clock
and the dark rose opens his scented bed.

The old man in his braces chewed a pipe
that smelt as strongly as a summer street,
dungsmoke or woodsmoke, gardens over-ripe
watered with bird-twitters, hazy with heat.

He thought the poetry he wrote was thin
and lost somehow in real life mysteries,
his hammer tapped at what was genuine
in the sheep-dust of remote villages,

while stilly in his ears sounded the same
eroded music, years *ante bellum*,
ruining darkness or unnourished flame,
the crumbling architecture, the dead drum.

Poets are obstinate. In art, he said
the man is silent and the image speaks.
The world was in the image as he wrote:
behind the world the silence of the world,
behind that silence the man was silent:
the stillness of the poet when he speaks
is in the image, and that is silent.
Nothing speaks but the stillness of the man.
How silently the ink moves on the page,
death is silent and life is more silent.

They are whipped by the wasps of breakfast time,
shamble upstairs to stare into the smoke
kippering the dust-covers of their books;
piano music is unnatural
and the lute song in the dead barber's shop
has melted away words, the heart is dust.
Whose dead weight has broken the dying grain.
These ragged old men in the hand of God
shaving by habit are not deserted
by the thin music that they have desired
and not deserted by the springing leaf
that peppers hedges, sprinkles the wet woods;
at their window they hear the fluting thrush.

When the wind smelling of burnt straw pulls out
the last of summer like a ruined tooth,
and the long shadows in the coarse air shout
to obscure birds they are singing the truth,
it is dreamtime for youth.

Youth sleeps heavy, and wakes only to doubts:
life is eaten away both ends with tears,
the stiff horse plunging on the roundabout
carries away dead summers from deaf ears,
and marks the turn of years.

The big wind blew him over on his arse,
worried at him, and chewed away his head:
he was easy, decent and working class,
now his country has used him, and he's dead.

I lived in slippers, the weather was fine
but I wrote verses disregarding it,
Latin machines like music, *judenrein*,
three autumn days and never felt my feet.

The old dog in his dreams squeaking like mice,
a snail indoors exploring up the stairs,
the after-smell of your pillow, the nice
arrangement of the river of your hairs:

take life and run with it is my wisdom,
poetry is about what you leave out:
the sun broods through the windows of a room,
what has survived is worth thinking about.

The Lakes at Blenheim

High branches drowse and the leaves press
against the dazzle of the sky
through water-vapours and greenness,
and plunge them into fire and light.

Only a sturdy sycamore
planted for shade and not for light:
for its companionable roar
in winter when the wind is high,

but now the tree's far higher than
the stone lodge: now the stream in spate
under the bridge's tiny span
hurls its green water in the lake.

These things are ducal, negligent,
a thousand geese swim on the lake,
and none of it was ever meant
to halt the obscure machine of fate.

The great leaf-banks of chestnut poise,
and will drop soon with little noise.
Mud-shallows. Birds are water-voiced,
boats blazing white, like Russian toys.

Austin, Texas

1

They say syntax is articulate energy,
I know art is intense energy,
here syntax is articulate lethargy,
and the sky vast, a sky renewed for me
where clouds run like fabulous cattle.
To be done then with poems short of breath.
The energy of the city is a machine,
the blood in arteries intensely pumps
like circulating oil, the light blazes
from oil consumed without any limit.
Homeric dawns and the star-lights of cars.
Desert enough elsewhere, puffs of pine trees
shelter the lucky poor. Nobody walks
away into the trees. Nobody goes.
Overhead at dawn aeroplanes ascend
in God's hand, and in falling light return.
No violin music, no water-noises:
just a few people took to the river
in whose heads only a fresh poem rings.

2

The afternoon sun blazes through damp,
it makes clarity, whole buildings glitter,
yet the green river smells of breweries:
art in my head, tremulous as a flag,
I walk in the thin shadows of the street
where long and sharp the heads of the dark birds
making rat whistles in magnolia trees
enjoin the scale of a heroic age:
senate-house or jail-house, the little stones.
But I fear the old people of this town
lining fences to jeer the volunteers:
there was no water to put out that fire
that burnt the jail-house and the senate-house.
And our last plight is worse than our first plight.
A coloured handkerchief flung on the breeze,
it trembles in the breeze and is dissolved.
Inside our galleries the sky refined,
by other skies infected, has no self:
rat whistles in the live-oak and the pine.

3

The hot air flops under the trees
and sunlight hangs like gilding
on leaf and branch or slides at ease
on a neoclassic building.

The noiseless lift, the marble stair
will lead you to such spoils
as Compton Mackenzie's writing chair
and Belloc-Lowndes in oils,

the whir and click of liberal brains,
lit eyes and silent sniggers
over the handwritten remains
of literary figures.

Tingling with knowledge we depart
to dream like Walter Mitty
of cooler streets, more lasting art
and some much smaller city.

Sarcastic whistling birds mark our
route past the monuments,
'from two to six the happy hour'
returns our life to sense.

The bearded faces, solemn eyes
harrowed with learned crazes
beam with an air of mild surprise
at girls as fresh as daisies.

We're happy in the oyster bar
talking of our dead nation,
wine-jugged and happier by far
than this sad celebration.

4

What is it after all, the individual
soul that wrings verses from the dripping moons,
harassed by ring-roads and confused by all
its settings-out melted to afternoons?

Calmed with cigar-smoke, feeding on autumn
twilight, field-mist inhabited by rooks
thousands of miles away, yet it is dumb
among the empty pages of notebooks.

It is the echo of another age,
life forgotten, not hoarded at all,
quite silent in the turning of a page,
quite effortlessly individual.

Texas long-horned cattle with silken coats
as pretty as a banner in a battle,
deep bony murmurs groaning in their throats:
only there are no Texas long-horned cattle.

Shimmering woods parade along the river
where boys with Indian skins like acrobats
loll in the shade and the weeds make you shiver,
and pairs of scullers whizz by in tall hats.

I fumigate myself with poetry
and lay my head down heavy on my pillow:
I give my fruit and root, but never see
a bone-shelled, burrowing Texas armadillo.

6

Art has flaunted an international flag
bold in provincial towns, the river-mouth
or river-bend, a tiny baroque swag,
our times have censored away the old south:

where whiskered senators in waggons brewed
their drinks and drank them at their waggon tails,
saw their sons killed in feud after failed feud
and paid dues in tobacco and in nails:

unable to afford the town hotels,
small houses built in purest neo-Greek:
our mind is tethered now in tall hotels,
fried in sun-dazzle, aired along the creek,

we live cocooned in fear and gravity,
there is no future and there was no past,
art being rootless, souls imaginary,
and complaint and lament quiet at last.

How far was it from here, great Alexander
stamping humans like trash, dead but bleeding,
ran through the inmost desert just to wander
into a wider Texas, and dying?

Birds screamed on the hot barrels of the guns,
herds of longhorns stampeded or went down
in pools of blood and steam to die when once
the Indians burned in their wooden town.

Iron rations now: the thin bugle cry,
dog-headed gods, vultures that flap in sand
to guard the unwatered desert where we die,
and the sour brooks afflict the poisoned land.

8

The windows flash
twenty-four storeys high,
weightless as ash
and sudden as a sigh;

a building in
a gleaming copper sheath
gyrates like sin
in a sundance with death,

those passing tread
the coarse grass of the south,
like lying dead
till seeds break in their mouth.

Tall buildings sigh
at evening in the light,
lovely and high
and for a moment bright:

pretend the sun
has lit his cigarette,
and our day's one
whose sun will never set.

Under the stunning crush of brilliant air
the grackle warbles, whistles, mildly flutes,
a pure enthusiast not for music
but Latin declamation built like stones,
vernacular background to the falls of kings,
crude as a starling shouts across highways
atropurpureus in his black notes.
There is no mind behind the eye of bronze
decorated with spectacles of bronze,
but mindless moral virtue, fortitude
and success shoring up our turpitude.
Dead quiet streets, courtesies of the south
counting aloud to wear our fingers out,
embodied in expensive bicycles.

10

The shadows of our handsome tall hotels
droop among bat-squeaks on the Alamo,
restored by ladies in old tennis shoes,
stone chapel roofless, the walls powder-scarred.
Virgin of the Alamo, the cottonwood tree,
enthroned on leaves in a desert of stones,
circled by noiseless rivers, by the roadless roads,
virgin of hot lead and of the hot wind,
lean quiet-handed over the dead men
make a garden with shadows for our south.
The tree has shivered, it weeps inwardly
in its own sappy wood, the scars are dry
and the white walls have crumbled in the sun.
Virgin of the Alamo
Virgin of the cottonwood tree

For Dom

The stony town did what it could
to make us shiver and write well,
we left it for the darkening wood
where heaven's stars hissed as they fell,

trembled and rose as ikon lamps
for sages (if they wrote at all)
as kind and destitute as tramps,
as townless, houseless, natural.

But you were gone before the end,
the gin river, the city death,
my innocent and early friend
whose first poems were dying breath:

while I invented a garden,
a town where no one was at home;
you had imagined India then
and I had shut my eyes to Rome.

Inside the skull a world away
the white swan's icy glittering
shrank to black in a winter's day,
the echo of a beating wing.

Death has consumed that faith to burn
as yellow in the orchard tree:
poetry's seasonal return
of natural immortality.

Now lost in your mythology,
a kind of backwards of belief,
I feel for walls and only see
your verses full of love and grief.

George Seferis in his twilight
saw a blue star and said to me,
Before I die I want to write
just a little bad poetry.

There is a truth I am certain
that is not otherwise expressed:
you know how little words contain,
I write you these and am at rest.

America of fantasy and loss,
neither the last nor the best hope of mankind
but a province in the kingdom of eros,
corrupt evening coolness of the crazed mind
where old jazz darkens the river's dark green
and grabs you unpredictably like young jazz
and hammers in the blood like gasoline
seeing no god to be as perfect as;
because the gods went down with the republic,
cartloads of carnage, decadence of bronze;
our corporation would have made them sick,
they were glamorous in shadows as we were once:
it is all eros, mankind's history:
drums cannons and flags carried unfurled
interrupted some long catastrophe
of eros, shady master of the world.

The copper beeches cast vermilion shade
beside the water, then still more intense
burnish to brown rags while the shadows wade
in the lake ripples, but they make no sense
or no more sense than autumn always did:
we were reduced at last by the long shine
of mornings in the mist, while the wind slid
through walls to batter down our perfect vine.
We have been standing at the end of time
and at the raw beginning of our fears,
we are pursued by the slow backward chime
of echoes from the clock, long in the ear,
till willy-nilly in that labyrinth
or crystal image of eternity
we creep to die: the Roman hyacinth
in spring scent is the sign we shall live by.

It is so loud, the roar of history,
so troublesome the noises in our life
added to daily by bleak radios,
recorded music never sounding right,
you do not hear the sheep-bells out of doors,
they tinkle from the vestments of the priests,
and military bands falling silent
create the quiet of another shore,
our new horizon is death or the past
or the small continuity of life
where we adjust without intending it
to bird-calls and the garden's subtle tones
and thin caresses of autumnal sun:
our republic a dream and derelict.
Gothic ruins make a sad conversation,
the Parthenon drowning in purple fog
the coast or ghost of youth and our intention
which was our future and a fantasy:
I fear that we have understood the world.

Le vent se lève, il faut tenter de vivre

The wind is rising, it is time to live,
then falling, it is time to be timeless,
patrol the garden carpeted with grass
and kick the fallen leaves of orchard trees:
O cold virginity in the slim trees
which are intoxicated with their smells,
noble corruptions of the sap and fruit.
I am disturbed in season by roses,
rescued by yellow leaf and lasting green
old grass being my mind's freshest lining.
Here like an antique god I stretch at ease
on grass toasting my skin with exercise
conceiving I will build an arch of stones,
only my goddess views it balefully
and the small timeless flowers come and go.

Under the chiselled hair the head is crisp,
and the body naked and confident
with pubic hair chiselled in ferny fronds,
the left hand resting lightly on the hip:
well, we have all seen metal worse misused,
and we have seen bodies of worse proportion,
the masque of muscles under normal skin
that tighten into bronze and slightly gleam
as if to say I am oiled, I am swift,
while the dust settles and the silken web
stirs in the dusty sunlight round the head.
Here stood a prince ready to be admired,
acting his part, irresolute and sad,
but the real man despised the metal man
and far away he wandered out of sight
transforming from a self into a death.

In the days when we have vanished
nobody will understand
that the future looked unfinished
unattractive and unplanned.

When the hot jam poured on puddings
and the kitchen smelt of meat
and the monks of Little Gidding
sat out smoking in the street,

when the beer and wine and whisky
lit a rainbow on the tongue,
otter-hunting wasn't nasty
and a soldier wasn't young,

when old faces peered from hedges
just the same as animals,
and the women looked like witches,
village-like and rough as walls,

we were closer to those early
birds that saw our race begin:
you can have the future Charley,
we shall not be moving in.

The souls of men scarcely exist although
they will exist or at moments they do
in conversations with eternity
forgotten, unrecorded, blurred by dreams:
Bach mutters in the strings of a cello,
and Shakespeare murmurs obscure poetry
about the virgin funerals of birds:
and the scytheman is darkened by the sun
and will stalk homeward hardly muttering
whose steel scythe whistled to the stony field.
Souls of women are in the orchard trees
whose linen is wind-dried on the high lines,
and in the hand of God they are fragile,
the muttering of men in cello strings
is as fragile, drowning in heaven's eye,
and the soul hangs in heaven, lost in them.

Unlit, apple-smelling, rose-blanketed
cottages astounding in August
with purple daisies, dahlias and red
hot pokers, mint and cabbages and dust,
that will pass on before us into life
being home-made like heaven's architecture,
two acres to a cottage, black plots rife
with every flowering weed that sniffs moisture,
and unknown to that monstrous second birth
which is to come and bestial and godlike,
creeping as still as blood to crust the earth
in cut stone mountains, bubble domes that break,
cellophane galleries where spiders run
chanting unearthly music to divine
shadows dropped on us by the ruined sun
at the dead point of history's decline.
Easy to prefer England to all that:
which is dying, has been dying, will die,
the sliding moment that the clock stopped at,
war after war, then the mature goodbye.

From the Terrace

White fireflies of jasmine swarm in the dark
like poetry no better than this line:
death is the view from the long silent lawn
where the blue jay still chitters in the pine.

The jasmine smells as cheap as lemonade,
far out in our garden an urn of stone
marks the old fantasy of some milord:
a few lines live, we are shadow and bone.

From this oak tree you see the upper Thames
mooning and trailing round the level land,
or here and there you catch a hint of it:
our landscape is far flatter than your hand.

The casual farm-houses stretching out
in peace hide behind screens of standing trees,
sour ditches and dry aromatic grass
invite death like unnavigated seas.

We live like older people, in ten years
our garden urn has toppled in the hay,
our last horizon is mere grass-meadows,
we live by poems that have had their day.